CW00539158

# Working together on firework displays

A guide to safety for firework display organisers and operators

**HSE Books**

© *Crown copyright 2006*

*First published 1995*
*Second edition 1999*
*Reprinted with amendments 2002*
*Third edition 2006*

**ISBN 0 7176 6196 2**

All rights reserved. No part of this publication may be reproduced, stored in a retrieval system, or transmitted in any form or by any means (electronic, mechanical, photocopying, recording or otherwise) without the prior written permission of the copyright owner.

Applications for reproduction should be made in writing to:
Licensing Division, Her Majesty's Stationery Office,
St Clements House, 2-16 Colegate, Norwich NR3 1BQ
or by e-mail to hmsolicensing@cabinet-office.x.gsi.gov.uk

This guidance is issued by the Health and Safety Executive. Following the guidance is not compulsory and you are free to take other action. But if you do follow the guidance you will normally be doing enough to comply with the law. Health and safety inspectors seek to secure compliance with the law and may refer to this guidance as illustrating good practice.

# Contents

# Foreword to third edition

Since the publication of *Working together on firework displays* in 2002 there have been significant changes in the statutory controls relating to the supply, possession, transport, keeping and use of fireworks which may have an effect on the way you organise and fire your display.

## The Manufacture and Storage of Explosives Regulations 2005[1]

These wide-sweeping Regulations replace a significant portion of the Explosives Act 1875 as well as revoking and amending a range of regulations. They impose duties on the manufacture and storage of explosives, including fireworks, as well as placing requirements for the prevention of fire and explosion. They are supported by guidance and an approved code of practice.[2]

## The Carriage of Dangerous Goods and Use of Transportable Pressure Equipment Regulations 2004[3]

These Regulations replaced a large number of statutory instruments relating to different transport modes. They implement the European agreements relating to road and rail transport (ADR and RID) providing a single, consolidated, set of regulatory measures.

## The Firework (Safety) Regulations 1997[4]
## The Firework (Safety) (Amendment) Regulations 2004[5]

These Regulations primarily address the supply of fireworks and include provisions relating to:

■ the prohibition of the sale to the general public of a variety of types of fireworks* such as:

- category 4 fireworks;
- aerial shells and maroons;
- shells-in-mortar and maroons-in-mortar;
- bangers, including batteries containing bangers and Chinese crackers;
- fireworks with erratic flight;
- mini-rockets;
- air bombs;

■ limits on the sizes of certain category 2 and 3 fireworks that can be supplied to the general public;
■ a requirement that fireworks of category 1, 2 and 3 conform with British Standard BS 7114: 1988[6]
■ an increase in the limit on the age of purchase to 18.

## The Firework Regulations 2004[7]

These Regulations include provisions relating to:

■ the prohibition of the possession of fireworks in public places by those under 18;
■ limitations on the times in the year during which fireworks may be supplied by unlicensed suppliers;
■ the control of the supply of certain types of excessively loud fireworks;
■ limitation on the use of fireworks during night hours.

You can get more information on these regulations on the Department of Trade and Industry website: **www.dti.gov.uk/fireworks**

You can download copies of the regulations from Her Majesty's Stationary Office website: **www.opsi.gov.uk/stat.htm**

* Some of these fireworks may still be supplied to certain people such as those in business as 'professional' firework display organisers and operators.

# Part 1: Guidance for display organisers

## Introduction

### *Who is this publication for?*

1    This publication gives advice on safety for outdoor firework displays where the fireworks are to be fired by a competent display operator (see paragraph 4 for a definition of this term). This edition provides an update on relevant legislation, training, risk assessment and competence. It does not cover displays where the fireworks are to be fired by people without specialised knowledge or training. Advice on safety for those displays can be found in *Giving your own firework display: How to run and fire it safely.*[8]

2    Firework displays typically fired by competent display operators vary widely in their nature and scale, for example:

- displays held around 5 November attracting thousands of spectators, often run by local authorities;
- displays held by businesses, for example to celebrate a special event, an invited audience where the number of spectators may be no more than a hundred or so, or open to the public;
- displays for celebrations such as weddings and birthdays.

3    The primary areas of interest to display **organisers** in this publication are in Parts 1, 3 and 4. The primary areas of interest to display **operators** are in Parts 2, 3 and 4. Display **operators** are strongly advised to be familiar with the rest of the publication. If display **organisers** are familiar with Part 2 it will help them understand the safety requirements of the display **operator**.

### *What is meant by a 'competent display operator'?*

4    A display operator should have sufficient knowledge, training and experience to set up and fire the fireworks and clear them up after firing in a way that ensures the health and safety of the operator, the operator's employees and other people at, or affected by, the display. Competence will normally be achieved through a combination of theoretical training (for example a 'classroom'-based training course), and practical 'on the job' training gained from planning, setting up and firing displays. It is not expected that satisfactory competence could be obtained without this practical training. The typical areas expected to be included in any training course are listed in Appendix 1.

A competent display operator will:

*understand:*

- the characteristics and proper use of the various types of fireworks, including debris patterns and fall-out distances;
- the principles and practice of ignition systems;
- the principles of carrying out a risk assessment;
- the principles and practice of setting up, firing and clearing up the fireworks both in relation to operator safety and the safety of others; and
- the requirements of health and safety legislation which apply to the activities of a firework display operator and firework displays;

*be trained in:*

- setting up, firing and clearing up fireworks, either by a competent display operator or as part of a training course;

*have practical experience in:*

- setting up, firing and clearing up fireworks under the supervision of a competent display operator;

*ensure:*

- that people forming part of a firing team who do not have knowledge, training or experience are directly supervised by an experienced team member.

5    Some display operators only use fireworks on sale to the general public which comply with BS 7114 Part 2: 1988, but more typically their displays will also include fireworks which are incomplete and/or not intended for sale to the general public (BS 7114 category 4). Not all display operators claim competence in using category 4 fireworks. It is very important that the operator should be competent for the fireworks to be used at your display. You should also be aware that the supply of fireworks is controlled by the Firework (Safety) Regulations 1997[4] and that certain types of fireworks, including some subject to BS 7114, may only be supplied to professional display operators.

## Organisation

### *General*

6    Useful guidance on the organising of a display can be obtained from *The event safety guide: A guide to health, safety and welfare at music and similar events.*[9]

*General legal considerations*

7   Most displays covered by this publication will involve a work activity (ie at least one person will be involved on a professional basis) and therefore be subject to the requirements of the Health and Safety at Work etc Act 1974[10] and subsidiary health and safety legislation. This legislation imposes duties in respect of the health and safety of everyone involved in arranging and giving the display, the display spectators, and other people in the neighbourhood of the display site.

8   You can only discharge these duties effectively if there is one person having overall responsibility for health and safety at the display. That person will usually be one of the organisers, and will be responsible for implementing a system for the management of health and safety to ensure the organisers, display operator and any other people working at the display, for example a catering firm, comply with their duties under health and safety legislation. In most cases, however, none of the organisers will be experts in setting up and firing fireworks and you are therefore advised to appoint a display operator to assist you with firework safety matters. Have a formal contract which defines the extent of responsibility of yourselves and the operator.

*Procedures*

9   Start organising the firework display as early as possible to ensure everything gets done. It is recommended that you form an organising team to share the workload, with one member in a co-ordinating role. For example, one person could be responsible for liaising with the display operator, local authority, fire service etc, another person for site facilities and crowd safety, and so on.

*Risk assessment*

10   The Management of Health and Safety at Work Regulations 1999[11] require employers to make a suitable and sufficient assessment of the health and safety risks to which their employees are exposed while at work, and the health and safety risks to other people resulting from or in connection with the employers' work. Information on risk assessment is given in Appendix 2.

## Defining the main features of the display

11   One of the first things to be done is to decide on some basic details, for example:

■   What is the expected size of the audience?
■   Is there to be a bonfire? (It is preferable not to light the bonfire before the fireworks are fired as stray sparks may accidentally set off the fireworks.)
■   Which display operator is to be contracted to fire the display?

## Selecting a display operator to fire the display

12   Careful selection of a display operator is important for the safety of people at the display.

13   The following points will assist you in selecting a display operator:

■   Can the operator provide evidence of competence as defined in paragraph 4?
■   What training and experience does the operator have? Is there any evidence of formal training?
■   Does the operator have insurance cover?
■   Does the operator agree to observe the safety recommendations in Parts 2, 3 and 4 of this publication?
■   Can the operator provide a list of displays he/she has fired in the past, together with the name of each display organiser?
■   Can the organisers of these earlier displays confirm there were no safety problems involving fireworks?
■   Where does the operator intend to obtain the fireworks? Is the source of supply a reputable company?
■   Has the operator asked to see the proposed site, or asked for details of it, before giving a quotation?
■   Has the operator taken the initiative in discussing responsibilities?

14   A list of addresses where you can obtain advice on the selection of a display operator is in Appendix 4.

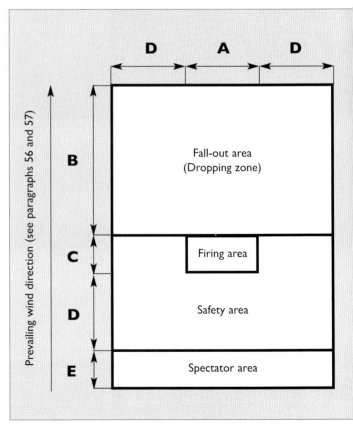

**Figure 1**  Site layout for displays (see paragraphs 16-23)

15 Once you have selected a display operator, you and the operator are strongly advised to agree your respective areas of responsibility for health and safety.

## Selecting a site for the display

*Definitions used in the text and in Figure 1*

16 The **display site** is the whole site used for the display, and is made up of:

■ the **spectator area** – from which the spectators watch the display;
■ the **safety area** – a clear area between the spectators and the firing area to ensure that spectators are at a safe distance from the fireworks during the display;
■ the **firing area** – from which the fireworks are set off;
■ the **fall-out area** (or dropping zone) – an area kept clear of people, where the debris from spent aerial fireworks lands; and
■ the **bonfire area** – the area provided for the bonfire (if there is to be one).

17 Figure 1 shows how these areas should be located in relation to each other and the prevailing wind direction.

18 The display site needs to be large enough to ensure all the above areas can cope with:

■ the types of fireworks to be used (this affects the size of the safety area and the fall-out area);

■ a change in the direction or strength of the wind;
■ the expected number of spectators.

19 The table in Figure 1 gives guidance on minimum dimensions. The safety distances given will be adequate in many cases, but the display operator may require greater distances for certain sizes or types of fireworks, for example crown wheels or flying saucers, or the larger sizes of shells. Allowance should be made for the burst diameter of shells when assessing safety distances. A 125 mm shell, for example, can project effects further than 50 metres and could therefore endanger spectators if it malfunctioned at ground level without sufficiently extended safety distances.

20 In special circumstances the safety distances given in the table may not always be appropriate, for example where displays are to be fired from unusual sites such as a barge on a river, the roof of a building, a bridge, or where only lancework or certain other non-aerial fireworks are to be used. In these cases it will be necessary for the operator to carefully assess the risks and decide on suitable spectator areas.

21 If you are using steel mortar tubes you should take account of hard surfaces such as car parks, buildings and bridges near the firing site which could cause the ricochet of steel fragments if mortar tubes fail. Ricochets can increase the distance travelled by fragments by as much as 30%.

22 Ensure the site is free of dry, cut grass and other readily combustible materials.

| | A | B | C | D | E |
|---|---|---|---|---|---|
| Minimum distance (metres) | 50 approx. | 100* | 25 | 50* | As required, to prevent overcrowding |

*The distances in columns B and D may have to be modified for certain types and sizes of firework

**Bonfire area** Locate this anywhere, provided it is:

■ at least 15 m from other areas, buildings, roads, railways and public rights of way;
■ a safe distance from flammable or otherwise dangerous materials (eg petrol, fuel oil, liquefied petroleum gas) and overhead electric power lines; and
■ downwind of spectators.

23 Only make the final selection of a site after you (and preferably the display operator) have inspected it in daylight to check for obstructions, eg trees, adjoining buildings and overhead power lines (Figure 2). Apart from obstructing the flight of aerial fireworks, overhead power lines pose other potential dangers, for example:

■ scaffolding poles, metal ladders and similar items used in the construction of temporary staging, or long wires such as those sometimes used in firing circuits for electrically fired fireworks, can cause a dangerous discharge of electricity from overhead power lines if they touch, or even come near to them. This is known as a 'flashover';
■ smoke or debris coming from fireworks or a bonfire burning under or near overhead power lines could also cause a flashover;
■ overhead electric power lines near to firing wires for electrically fired fireworks can induce an electric current in the wires, causing the premature firing of the fireworks.

24 If you are in any doubt about overhead electric power lines, contact the local regional electricity company for advice. If it is impossible to arrange the site so the firing and bonfire areas are well away from obstructions, you may need to look for another site. In some cases the display operator may advise that certain types of fireworks you have requested cannot be fired safely at your chosen display site.

## Who to contact

25 It is advisable to contact the following well before the display and keep in touch as your plans proceed. Reconfirm your arrangements on the day of the display:

### Police

26 Contact the police as soon as possible, informing them of the location of the site and its layout, including all entrances and exits.

27 The police's main interests are crowd control, public order, emergency access, and local traffic management and parking. It is advisable to act on any recommendations they make.

### Fire service

28 Contact the fire service at least 28 days before the event. They will mainly be interested in:

■ how the emergency services will be called;
■ access for emergency vehicles;
■ marshalling crowds and traffic in emergency conditions;
■ arrangement of spectators' enclosures;
■ local fire-fighting arrangements; and
■ buildings and other features nearby which could be affected by a fire.

Figure 2  Inspecting the site (see paragraph 23)

### Local authority

29 You may need to contact the local authority under entertainments and related legislation (see Appendix 3). In any case think about contacting:

■ local authority enforcement officers, for advice on complying with health and safety legislation and other matters such as minimising noise nuisance, avoiding any problems that may have occurred in the past, and complying with local by-laws;
■ the trading standards/environmental health departments, or in some areas the fire service, if you are in any doubt about arrangements for storing fireworks before the display. The place of keeping may need to be licensed or registered under the Manufacture and Storage of Explosives Regulations 2005.[1]

### Local institutions

30 It is wise, in the interests of good public relations, to inform any local hospitals, old people's homes etc of the event.

### Neighbouring landowners or users

31  Advance warning to neighbouring landowners or users at an early stage will enable them to move livestock (cattle, horses etc) where necessary.

32  Local people likely to be affected by the display may not be aware of it through local advertising. Contacting them via a leaflet drop, for example, would be preferable to leaving them unaware of the nature, scale, timing and duration of the event.

### Coastguard

33  If the display is to be held near the sea it is important to inform the local coastguard in advance. Aerial fireworks could be mistaken for distress signals.

### Harbour authority

34  Inform the harbour authority as soon as possible, and at least 24 hours in advance, if the display is to be anywhere in a harbour area, or if the fireworks have to be taken through a harbour area to reach the display site. Under the Dangerous Substances in Harbour Areas Regulations 1987,[12] there is a duty to give advance notice of the entry of dangerous goods into a harbour area.

### Aerodromes

35  If the display is to be held near an aerodrome, inform the airport authority at least seven days in advance. Alternatively, contact the Civil Aviation Authority (CAA), Safety Regulation Group, Aviation House, Gatwick Airport South, West Sussex RH6 0YR Tel: 01293 567171, particularly if you are unsure whether there are aerodromes near the display site. Adhere to height restrictions for aerial fireworks stipulated by the airport authority or CAA. The Civil Aviation Authority has issued detailed guidance on the operation of lasers, searchlight and fireworks in UK Airspace[13] (CAP 736). This document can be downloaded from the CAA web site (www.caa.co.uk) or requested from the address given above.

36  If you are unsure whether or not to get in touch with anyone – do so.

## Provision of site facilities

37  Prevent spectator access to the safety, fall-out, bonfire and display areas, by a suitable form of physical barrier.

38  Check that fire-fighting facilities at the site are adequate and consider asking the fire service or a fire-fighting specialist for advice. The following provisions are advised as a minimum:

- equipment for putting out small fires (eg fire extinguishers, buckets of water, fire blankets) available throughout the display site; and
- an adequate number of stewards instructed in how to use this equipment. Tell the stewards not to attempt to fight major fires.

39  Provide at least two spectator exits from the site which are large enough, spaced well apart, clearly marked, kept free from obstructions and well lit.

40  Keep the agreed emergency service routes clear of obstruction and readily accessible at all times.

41  A small public address system or loudspeaker will ensure that announcements and instructions can be clearly heard by all spectators at larger displays.

42  Provide at least one suitably equipped first-aid point, manned by a qualified first-aider. Signpost it clearly and make it easily accessible to an ambulance.

43  Provide suitable litter receptacles throughout the spectator area.

44  Any car-parking area should preferably be well away from the display site and upwind of it (ie with the wind blowing from the car park towards the site). Do not allow parking anywhere else. The parking area needs to be clearly signposted, with vehicle and pedestrian routes to and from the parking area totally segregated from each other. Where appropriate, supervise parking to prevent obstruction of emergency access routes.

45  Locate any bar selling alcohol well away from the display site and do not allow alcohol to be taken away from the bar area. No one involved in running the display should be under the influence of intoxicating substances.

## Looking after the fireworks before the display

46  It is advisable for the display operator to be responsible for keeping the fireworks at all times, because the operator will:

- already have a safe and suitable place of storage; and
- know how to transport the fireworks by road from the storage place to the display site in accordance with the relevant legislation listed in Part 4.

47  Provide a safe place at the display site to store fireworks immediately before use, for example a building or a closed metal or wooden container located in an area of the site not accessible to the public. Alternatively, they can be kept in the display operator's vehicle parked in an area not accessible to the public, provided they are kept safely.

48  Once fireworks have been set up, ensure the firing area is supervised.

## Crowd safety

49  Provide an adequate number of stewards responsible solely for crowd safety. Ensure stewards receive adequate briefing, and a clear chain of command exists. Make them easily identifiable, for example they could all wear fluorescent jackets (Figure 3). Instruct them to be on constant watch for emergencies.

**Figure 3** A steward responsible for crowd safety (see paragraphs 49-53)

50 Pay particular attention to keeping spectators out of the safety, firing and fall-out areas. Control entry to the spectator area to avoid overcrowding.

51 Do not admit spectators to the display with their own fireworks. Publish proper notice of this in advance and post notices at all the entrances. No fireworks should be on sale at the site.

52 Make every effort to start the display on time as crowd control becomes more difficult, the longer people are kept waiting. If a delay is unavoidable, tell the spectators and ask for their co-operation at an early stage.

53 Some important points on crowd safety can be found in the leaflet *Managing crowds safely: A guide for organisers at events and venues.*[14]

## What if something goes wrong?

### Plan in advance!

54 Well before the day of the display, you will need to consider what could go wrong on the day. Draw up a plan to deal with each emergency or contingency, answering the questions 'What action will be taken?' and 'Who will take that action?' Involve the display operator in this exercise where necessary.

55 Paragraphs 56-62 highlight some of the problems which could arise, and actions which could be taken. The

list is not exhaustive, but should help you plan ahead for emergencies.

### Stopping the display early or cancelling it due to adverse wind conditions

56 You will have based the layout of the display site on the prevailing wind direction (see Figure 1). If the wind direction is different on the day of the display, the display operator may suggest modifying the layout to ensure people's safety. If this is impossible or inadvisable for other reasons, for example because this would interfere with exits, consider the actions described for high winds in paragraph 57.

57 In high winds it may be necessary to modify the display (eg eliminate aerial fireworks) or, in extreme conditions, cancel it or finish early. Involve the display operator in these decisions; do not continue if the operator advises cancelling or stopping the display.

### Accident to someone from a firework or incident involving a firework

58 Have a procedure to ensure that first-aiders have clear access to the injured person as soon as possible. In the case of serious injury, have an ambulance called immediately by a designated organiser and suspend firing of the display.

59 Where an accident or incident is reportable under the Reporting of Injuries, Diseases and Dangerous Occurrences Regulations 1995,[15] the enforcing authority should be

contacted as soon as possible and not later than legally required. Ensure the scene of the accident or incident is preserved and the remains of any fireworks involved and other debris are left undisturbed, unless this would pose an immediate threat to safety. The enforcing authority will tell you when you may start clearing up.

### Bonfire out of control or fire started by firework debris

60   If you cannot deal with the fire immediately, using first-aid fire-fighting equipment, call the fire service without delay. Instruct the display operator to suspend firing of the display until the fire is extinguished or the fire service advises it is under control. You may need to move spectators to a safe place away from the site of the fire, but ensure that a clear access route for the fire appliance is maintained at all times.

### Spectators in the safety, firing or fall-out areas

61   If spectators break through the barrier into the safety, firing or fall-out areas, ensure that firing of fireworks stops as soon as is practicable.

### Disorderly behaviour by spectators

62   If trouble seems to be developing, call the police before attempting to deal with the matter yourselves.

### Announcements to spectators

63   Prepare announcements in advance which can be made to the spectators in the event of an emergency, telling them what has happened and what they are required to do.

### Communications

64   It is advisable to have a two-way radio link between the display operator and those with key responsibilities for emergency action. At large-scale events it is preferable to have several channels operating, eg control to stewards; control to firework crew; firework crew to musicians/producer etc. Have an agreed procedure on radio for dealing with emergencies (Figure 4).

## Bonfires

65   Make one person responsible for the bonfire, and allow only that person and designated helpers into the bonfire area. **Do not use petrol or paraffin to light the fire.** A safer way to light is to use paper and solid firelighters in two or three places to ensure an even burn. Do not burn dangerous rubbish such as foam-filled furniture, rubber, aerosols, tins of paint, pressurised gas cylinders, tyres and bottles. Materials producing light ash which could blow about, such as corrugated cardboard, are unsuitable for burning.

**Figure 4** Communications (see paragraph 64)

66   Before lighting the fire, check its construction carefully to make sure it is stable, and that there are no children or animals inside (Figure 5).

67   The people looking after the bonfire are advised not to wear lightweight clothing which could ignite relatively easily. They are recommended to wear a substantial outer garment of wool or other material of low flammability and strong boots or shoes. They need to know what to do in the event of a burn injury or a person's clothing catching fire, and also have a fire blanket ready in the bonfire area.

**Figure 5** Checking the bonfire before lighting (see paragraph 66)

# Part 2: Guidance for display operators

## Setting up and firing the fireworks

68  The operations described in this part of the guidance should only be carried out by display operators or their staff.

### Risk assessment

69  The Management of Health and Safety at Work Regulations 1999[11] require employers to make a suitable and sufficient assessment of the health and safety risks to which their employees are exposed while at work, and the health and safety risks to other people resulting from or in connection with the employers' work. Information on risk assessment is given in Appendix 2.

### What type of fireworks will the display operator use?

70  Fireworks used by display operators usually include BS 7114 category 4 fireworks (see paragraph 5). These typically have little labelling on them. They often do not have complete fuse systems and are often used by display operators as components linked together by fusing to create larger fireworks. Because of this it is not practicable for manufacturers or suppliers to provide detailed instructions on setting up and firing these fireworks. Some category 4 fireworks are much larger and more powerful than those available to the general public, and are potentially more hazardous.

## Setting up category 4 fireworks

### General precautions

71  Display operators are advised to take the following precautions.

- Do not smoke when handling fireworks, or in the firing area once fireworks are present.
- Where fireworks are tied to stakes or other supports, tie them on the side facing away from the audience. Then, if a malfunction occurs and the firework falls over, it is probable that any remaining projectiles or effects will fall away from the audience.

### Instructions

72  Conditions for the authorisation of fireworks in Great Britain require that suitable markings and instructions are provided with fireworks, giving clear advice on the safe method of their handling, storage and use.

73  Suppliers or manufacturers usually provide an instruction leaflet with the fireworks on how to use them safely. Read it well in advance of the display, and contact the supplier, manufacturer or importer with any queries. Follow the instructions closely during setting up and firing.

### Firing plan

74  It is advisable to prepare a firing plan well before the fireworks are set up.

### Fusing

75  The setting up of category 4 fireworks may involve the modification or completion of fusing at the firing area. Aim to complete work of this type well before spectators arrive. When fusing is in progress, limit access to the firing area to the display operator and those carrying out the fusing. Keep any members of the public at a safe distance. Carry out fusing in daylight or, failing this, under suitable artificial lighting.

76  Manipulation of fusing presents a potential for accidental ignition. The following safety points are particularly important.

- Cut fusing by a method which does not cause sparks, eg using a sharp pair of clippers or scissors with cutting edges made of a non-sparking material, or a sharp knife on a cutting surface of non-sparking material. You are advised to contact the manufacturer or supplier of the fuse for guidance on the recommended method of cutting any specific products.
- Never tear fusing apart or use a blunt instrument or saw to cut it.
- Never expose electric igniters to sources of friction such as rough insertion into, or removal from, blackmatch.
- Make all joins so that they leave no exposed composition and are strong enough to withstand the stresses they will experience (Figure 6). Tape all joints if necessary.
- Hold the fuse in position by a method which will neither generate sparks while the fuse is being secured, nor damage it in any way. Plastic ties or adhesive tape are recommended (Figure 7). Do not staple fusing directly into place using staple guns or similar devices. Staple guns should only be used to fix cable ties or similar which are then used to secure the fusing.
- When joining different types of fuses, do not bring incompatible materials in contact with each other, eg sulphur and chlorates.

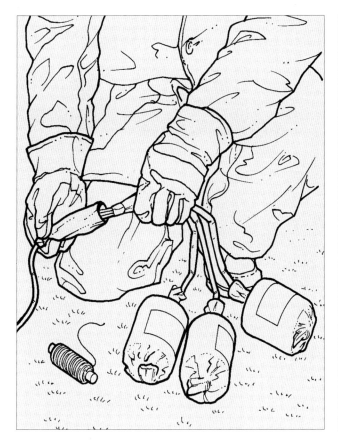

**Figure 6** Joining a fuse (see paragraph 76)

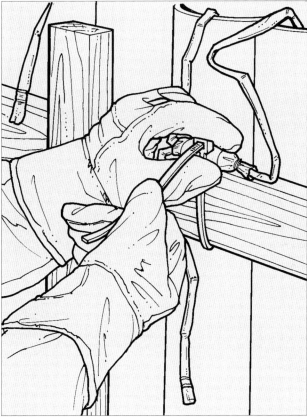

**Figure 7** Securing a fuse by a plastic tie (see paragraph 76)

■ Fuseheads may be easily ignited by friction, crushing or cutting and should be handled with care.

77 The above guidance relates only to the fusing of fireworks before use. The dismantling of fused fireworks or firework assemblies is a more complex undertaking requiring careful selection of procedures and may require special facilities.

78 When many fireworks are grouped or fused together, the potential for accidental ignition is greatly increased. Ensure boxes of firework sequences are not left open. Put fusing in a safe place and cover it to minimise the risk of accidental ignition from stray sparks etc. Keep the number of fireworks being worked on to a minimum, and keep the remainder covered or in closed boxes.

*The use of support tubes*

79 The use of support tubes is not a preferred method of support and, in any case, may only be suitable for static fireworks such as roman candles, fountains, mines and shot tubes.

80 Where the fireworks concerned are in category 2 or 3, always follow the firing instructions provided. Tubes should not be used to support these categories of fireworks unless they have been supplied for specific use with the firework, for example rocket launch tubes.

81 For category 4 fireworks, the use of support tubes is not necessary – there are a variety of better, alternative methods of support. However, if support tubes must be used, please take the following simple precautions:

■ Do not use metal tubes. Consider using only plastic tubes which, should the firework explode unexpectedly, will not burst, shedding high-energy fragments. Choose tubing which is made of non-brittle plastic and designed to withstand internal pressure, for example pipe made for water or gas supplies, from high-density polyethylene (HDPE).

■ Do use a tube with a diameter which will provide the required support to the firework without holding it too snugly. A snug tube may damage the firework when it is inserted and also increase the severity of a misfire.

■ Where any support tube is attached to a stake or frame, attach it on the side away from the spectators. In this way, should an explosion occur, the effects will tend to be projected away from the spectators.

■ Always remember to position fireworks as far as possible from spectators and at least the manufacturer's recommended minimum distance. Where specific safety distances are not provided, you should refer to information on the minimum recommended safety distances in Figure 1.

■ In any event, your arrangements for fastening, supporting and locating the fireworks should be justified in your risk assessment.

*Maroon rockets*

82   Avoid firing maroon rockets from a rocket cone or firing box. Cones may be used for other types of rockets provided their heads are clear of the cone.

*Shells*

83   Use shells with the utmost care. Ensure you are familiar with the type of shell you are using and ensure you have read and understood the warnings and instructions supplied with the shell and mortar tube.

84   The main problems with firing a shell from a mortar tube arise where the shell:

- is not projected correctly because the mortar tube has toppled over;
- bursts at a low height. This can happen when an incorrect mortar tube diameter or length is used, or when the shell is not lowered to the bottom of the mortar tube;
- bursts in the mortar tube due to malfunction. This may cause the mortar tube to burst and project fragments, and adjacent mortar tubes may be disrupted;
- bursts at the mouth of the mortar tube on ejection. In this case it is likely the mortar tube is not fragmented, but stars and shell debris will be scattered around the immediate area;
- ignites prematurely where the fuse was not ignited at its tip.

85   You are strongly advised to remember the following basic rules when using mortar tubes.

- Ensure mortar tubes are of the correct diameter and length for the shell.
- Do not use undue force when inserting a shell into a mortar tube. The mortar tube dimensions and condition should allow the shell to be lowered smoothly to rest on the bottom of the mortar tube.

- Mortar tubes must not be free-standing.
- Preferably avoid firing maroons from racked mortar tubes.
- When mortar tubes are racked together, support them with a firmly fixed sturdy frame, eg by wooden stakes, so they cannot topple over (Figure 8a).
- Bury or sandbag single mortar tubes deep enough to prevent them toppling over, and inclined away from spectators (Figures 8b-d). Take precautions to ensure a misfire in one mortar tube will not disrupt other mortar tubes.
- Do not fire single shot maroons from metal mortar tubes.
- Ensure mortar tubes are strong and durable enough for the shells. When deciding whether the mortar tube material should be cardboard, plastic or metal, think about using a material that would not fragment or produce hazardous debris if a shell malfunctioned in the mortar tube. If a mortar tube is made of material which could produce hazardous debris, sandbag or barricade it. Use enough sandbags or barricading to ensure firers and spectators would be protected if a shell malfunctioned in the mortar tube. Research suggests that you may get better protection from hazard debris if sandbags or protective barricades are in contact with the mortar tubes. An air gap between the mortar tubes and the barricade will reduce the effectiveness of the protection.
- Always clean out mortar tubes and check they are reasonably dry before use.
- Ensure mortar tube bungs are held firmly in place and checked before firing each display.
- Preferably avoid reloading mortar tubes during a display. Where mortar tubes are reloaded, group them according to size to help avoid shell/mortar tube mismatches.

a) Firmly fixing a mortar tube frame

b) Burying single mortar tubes (step 1)

c) Burying single mortar tubes (step 2)

d) Burying single mortar tubes (step 3)

**Figure 8**  Preparing mortar tubes (see paragraph 85)

# Firing the display

## *Protective clothing and equipment*

86   Firers are advised to wear substantial outer clothing made of wool or some fire-retardant material such as probanised cotton. They are also recommended to wear gloves, safety goggles, safety helmets and substantial closed footwear made of leather or similar material (Figure 9).

87   Firers are advised to wear ear protectors or other suitable hearing protection. Where the firers are at work, the Control of Noise at Work Regulations 2005[16] will apply. This means display operators have to assess the exposures of employees and themselves to noise during firing, and where necessary take adequate measures to protect their hearing from damage (Figure 9). For electric firing, it may be possible to site the firing point far enough away from the fireworks for noise exposure to be below the action levels given in the Regulations. In this case ensure that firers retire to that point whenever firing is in progress.

## *Firing procedures*

88   It is important that the activities of the firing team are co-ordinated to ensure that everyone is in a safe position whenever fireworks are about to go off. Firers should be at least ten metres away from ground maroons.

89   If a mortar tube is to be reloaded with a shell, clear it of smouldering debris before a further shell is inserted.

90   Take any mortar tube showing signs of distortion, dangerous corrosion or damage out of use immediately.

## *Misfires*

91   Leave a firework which fails to ignite for at least 30 minutes. In most cases, it will then be best to immerse it in a bucket of water. Never position any part of the body over a misfired firework. In the particular case of a shell in a mortar tube, never look down the mortar tube and do not pull a shell out of the mortar tube by its fuse. Leave the shell in the mortar tube for at least 30 minutes before proceeding as follows.

■   Cut off any fuse which is hanging outside the mortar tube by the method described in paragraph 76 to prevent any possibility of 'hang fire' reigniting the fuse.
■   Prepare for tipping the mortar tube over by removing any sandbags or earth (in the case of a buried mortar), or releasing the mortar tube frame from its fixings. Take particular care to ensure no part of the body is over the mouth of the mortar tube during this operation.
■   Where practical, tip the shell out of the mortar directly into a bucket of water. If this is not practical, flush the mortar tube containing the shell with water before tipping the shell gently onto the ground. In both cases, ensure the mortar tube is pointing away from the body during tipping.

92   Further advice on the disposal of misfires is given in Part 3.

**Figure 9** Firer wearing protective clothing, safety goggles and ear protectors (see paragraphs 86-87)

# Part 3: Clearing up after the display

93 The following procedures are recommended as a practical arrangement for co-ordinating the work of the organisers and display operators in clearing up the display site, but are not intended to define all responsibilities.

## Organisers

■ keep the firing, safety and fall-out areas free of spectators until the display operator has had time to clear up, and locate and retrieve fireworks that have misfired;

■ arrange for the whole site, apart from the firing area, to be carefully checked for partly spent fireworks and other hazardous remains, and inform the display operator of any problems;

■ arrange for at least one organiser to return to the site at first light to make sure that it is clear of partly spent fireworks and other hazardous remains. If hazardous material is found, contact the display operator for advice on its disposal;

■ ensure the bonfire is completely extinguished and keep spectators out of the bonfire area until this has been done.

## Display operators

■ are responsible for clearing up the firing area and leaving it in a safe condition on the day of the display (Figure 10);

■ destroy misfires and partly spent fireworks at the display site wherever possible, and come prepared to carry out their destruction in accordance with the recommendations contained in *Disposal of explosives waste*.[17] It may be necessary to enlist the help of the organisers to keep everybody at a safe distance while destroying fireworks. It is advisable to discuss this with the organisers before the display. Do not transport partly spent fireworks or misfires away from the site on public roads, unless you are satisfied that you can do so in accordance with legal requirements (see Part 4);

■ advise the organisers on how to deal with partly spent fireworks or misfires which may be found after the display operator has left the site.

Figure 10  Clearing up the firing area after the display

# Part 4: Legal requirements

94  General advice on the application of health and safety legislation and responsibilities is given in paragraphs 7 and 8. Paragraphs 95-104 cover some requirements of other sections of the HSW Act and other health and safety legislation which is of particular relevance to firework displays, and should be read by organisers and display operators.

95  The text in paragraph 96 relates to self-employed people and may be of importance to you. Although only the courts can give an authoritative interpretation of law, in considering the application of this guidance to people working under another's direction, the following should be considered.

96  If people working under the direction and control of others are treated as self-employed for tax and national insurance purposes, they are nevertheless treated as employees for health and safety purposes. It may therefore be necessary to take appropriate action to protect them. If any doubt exists about who is responsible for the health and safety of a worker, this could be clarified and included in the terms of a contract. However, remember that a legal duty under section 3 of the HSW Act cannot be passed on by means of a contract, and there will still be duties towards others under section 3 of the HSW Act. If such workers are employed on the basis that they are responsible for their own health and safety, legal advice should be sought before doing so.

97  The two requirements detailed below, coupled with the requirement for a risk assessment explained in Appendix 2, are closely related and can be considered together:

- Section 2.2(a) of the HSW Act requires employers to provide and maintain plant and systems of work that are, so far as is reasonably practicable, safe and without risks to health.
- Section 3 of the HSW Act requires employers to conduct their undertakings in such a way that, so far as is reasonably practicable, people who are not employees are not exposed to health and safety risks. It also imposes a similar duty on the self-employed towards themselves and other people.

98  Where any event involves a work activity, the person who is providing the premises for the event may also have duties under section 4 of the HSW Act in relation to people other than their employees.

99  The Manufacture and Storage of Explosives Regulations 2005 require that the manufacture of fireworks (which includes dismantling them) shall only take place in a licensed factory. The Regulations allow the preparation, assembly, disassembly and fusing of firework displays at the place of intended use without a factory license. The Regulations also allow the preparation, assembly and fusing of fireworks, in quantities of no more than 10 kilograms at a time, at a site in relation to which a person holds a licence or registration for the storage of explosives, for the purposes of a firework display to be put on by that person. The destruction of fireworks in a safe manner does not require a factory licence.

100  Under the Manufacture and Storage of Explosives Regulations 2005, an unlimited quantity of hazard type 3 and 4 fireworks may be kept for up to 24 hours without licensing or registering the place of storage. Specified amounts may be held for longer periods without licensing or registration as shown in the table.

| Type of fireworks | Maximum amount (kg) | Maximum storage period (days) | Condition |
|---|---|---|---|
| Hazard type 3 | 100 | 3 | In place of intended use |
| Hazard type 4 | 250 | 3 | In place of intended use |
| Hazard type 4 | 50 | 21 | Not for sale or use at work |

**Table 1**  Amounts of fireworks which may be kept without licensing or registration

101  The transport of fireworks and other explosives by road is subject to the requirements of:

- The Classification and Labelling of Explosives Regulations 1983,[18] as amended by The Carriage of Dangerous Goods and Use of Transportable Pressure Equipment Regulations 2004;[3]
- The Carriage of Dangerous Goods and Use of Transportable Pressure Equipment Regulations 2004.

102  Some guidance on the carriage of dangerous goods by road is given in *Working with ADR: an introduction to the carriage of dangerous goods by road*.[19]

103  The above list of health and safety legislation is far from exhaustive. People who are responsible for health and safety at the display and those who are providing premises are recommended to consult the local authority enforcement officer for advice if they are in any doubt as to the application of health and safety legislation.

104  Information on legislation, other than health and safety legislation, which may apply to firework displays is given in Appendix 3.

# Appendix 1 Training courses

This list is not exhaustive but simply provides an indication of what a training course should typically include:

- The various types of fireworks available to professional firework operators, their effects (including duration, burst height etc), debris pattern and potential risks.
- Basic risk assessment including assessment and mitigation of risks.
- Site planning including layout, effects of wind and weather, special requirements of unusual sites etc.
- The nature of firing areas, safety area and fall-out area in relation to the overall display site, together with constraints or opportunities that might present themselves.
- Methods of modifying show content at the display site to reduce risk, eg repositioning aerial items, removing items, cancelling the display.
- Firing area layout.
- Fusing methods.
- Ignition systems – advantages and disadvantages.
- 'Rigging' – including aspects of unusual sites.
- General legal aspects including duties under the HSW Act etc.
- Specific legal duties including those involved with manufacture, storage, transport and disposal of fireworks.
- Basic display design.
- Basic first aid.
- Clearing up after the display.

# Appendix 2 Risk assessment

1    Regulation 3 of the Management of Health and Safety at Work Regulations 1992 requires employers to make a suitable and sufficient assessment of:

■    the health and safety risks to which their employees are exposed while at work; and
■    the health and safety risks to other people resulting from or in connection with the employers' work, to identify the measures needed to comply with health and safety legislation. The same duty is placed on self-employed people in respect of their own health and safety and that of other people.

2    Both the display operator and the display organiser should prepare a risk assessment. The display operator's assessment will form a part of the display organiser's overall risk assessment.

3    General guidance on risk assessment is given in the HSE leaflet *Five steps to risk assessment*.[20] For a firework display you would need to do the following:

■    identify the hazards;
■    identify who might be harmed and how;
■    evaluate the risks;
■    identify appropriate and adequate precautions; and
■    record the findings.

4    For the **display operator** the risk assessment need only cover the display itself and anything that might affect it. The **display organiser** needs to take account of every aspect of the event including any additional activities, such as the sale of refreshments, crowd control, access for the emergency services etc.

5    It is particularly important to consider the following:

*Display site location and layout* (see paragraphs 16-24):

■    Is the layout and size of the firing area adequate, bearing in mind the risk of the burning debris from one firework accidentally setting off another firework and endangering people and property, prevailing weather conditions, and the need for firers to be able to move safely out of the area etc?
■    Are the safety distances adequate for the fireworks to be fired, taking into account the risks from the malfunction of those fireworks and other eventualities?

*Setting up the fireworks* (see paragraphs 68-85):

■    Are the precautions to be taken while setting up the fireworks adequate, taking into account risks to those doing the work and other people, including the general public?
■    Have the risks to people from the possible problems arising with shells and other fireworks which can explode violently, or which project debris, been fully considered, and adequate precautions taken?

*Firing and clearing up* (see paragraphs 86-93):

■    Have the risks associated with these operations for your display been fully considered and adequate precautions taken?

# Appendix 3 Other legislation which may apply to firework displays

(The requirements in this appendix are not requirements under health and safety legislation.)

1    The information which follows has been supplied by representatives of organisations responsible for enforcement and is only a brief guide to some of the main provisions other than health and safety legislation which firework display organisers will need to consider. The appropriate organisation will be able to advise on how these and other related provisions apply to an individual case.

## Entertainments licensing and statutory controls on noise nuisance

### England and Wales

2    The public entertainments provisions of the Local Government (Miscellaneous Provisions) Act 1982[21] allow local authorities to control events such as pop festivals and open-air entertainments of which music forms a substantial part.

3    Public entertainment licensing is carried out by the district or metropolitan council. Enquiries must be made at least 28 days before the event in order to comply with the notification procedures. To allow public entertainment to be carried out without a licence is an offence which can carry severe penalties.

4    In licensing events, the enforcing authority can impose conditions for securing the safety of performers and anyone else present at the entertainment, and for preventing people in the neighbourhood from being unreasonably disturbed by noise. It will be a condition of the licence that any recommendations made to the enforcing authority by the police and fire brigade are complied with.

5    If the local authority has adopted the Private Places of Entertainment (Licensing) Act 1967,[22] similar conditions may be imposed on similar types of entertainment held on private premises, including those in the open air. This is to cover private clubs etc where admission is restricted to members (ie the general public are not admitted). The licensing function is dealt with in exactly the same way as above, but extends the controls to private entertainment provided for private gain.

6    Displays which are not subject to licensing under the above legislation will still be subject to legislation relating to noise nuisance, enforced by the environmental health department of the district or metropolitan council.

### Scotland

7    Public entertainments licensing is carried out by the district or regional council.

8    Where a firework display involves the use of premises as a place of public entertainment, some councils will require an application to be made for a Public Entertainment Licence under section 41 of the Civic Government (Scotland) Act 1982[23] and, as a condition of licence, may require the organisers to consult with the local fire authority and the police. In the Act, the term 'place of public entertainment' is defined (subject to certain exclusions) as any place where, on payment of money or goods to the same value, members of the public are admitted or may use any facilities for the purposes of entertainment or recreation.

9    Some councils require charitable organisations which hold public firework displays to seek permission for the display irrespective of whether an entrance fee is to be levied or not.

10    Comments on noise nuisance are as for England and Wales in paragraph 6 above.

## Firework displays near aerodromes

11    The Civil Aviation Authority has issued detailed guidance on the operation of lasers, searchlight and fireworks in UK Airspace[13] (CAP 736). This document can be downloaded from the CAA website (www.caa.co.uk) or obtained using the contact details given in paragraph 35.

# **Appendix 4** Sources of information on firework manufacturers, suppliers and display operators

The British Pyrotechnists Association (BPA),
8 Aragon Place, Kimbolton, Huntingdon,
Cambridgeshire PE28 0JD
Tel: 01480 861975
www.bpa-fmg.org.uk

The Confederation of British Industry,
Explosives Industry Group (CBI/EIG), Centre Point,
103 New Oxford Street, London WC1A 1DU
Tel: 020 7395 8063
www.cbi.org.uk

The Institute of Explosives Engineers (IExpE),
Cranfield University, RMCS Shrivenham,
Swindon, Wiltshire SN6 8LA
Tel: 01793 785322
www.iexpe.org

The Event Services Association (TESA),
Picton House, Lower Church Street,
Chepstow, Monmouthshire NP16 5XT
Tel: 01291 628103
www.tesa.org.uk

Local Authorities Coordinators of
Regulatory Services (LACORS),
10 Albert Embankment,
London SE1 7SP
Tel: 020 7840 7200
www.lacors.gov.uk

The Chief Fire Officers' Association,
9-11 Pebble Close, Amington, Tamworth,
Staffordshire B77 4RD
Tel: 01827 302300
www-old.cfoa.org.uk

The British Fireworks Association (BFA)
Mr J Woodhead, Cosmic Fireworks Ltd,
Fauld Industrial Estate, Tutbury,
Burton on Trent DE13 9HS
www.b-f-a.org

# Acknowledgements

*HSE gratefully acknowledges the participation of the following in the drafting and updating of this publication:*

The British Pyrotechnists Association
The Confederation of British Industry, Explosives Industry Group
Black Cat Fireworks Limited
Kimbolton Fireworks Limited
Le Maitre Fireworks Limited
Theatre of Fire
Theatrical Pyrotechnics Limited
Sam Woodward Pyrotechnics and Fireworks
SaxtonSmith Enterprises
The Consumer Safety Unit of the Department of Trade and Industry

*and help given by the following:*

Civil Aviation Authority
Maritime and Coastguard Agency
City and District of St Albans District Council
North Yorkshire Fire and Rescue Service
Lothian and Borders Fire Brigade
Solar Pyrotechnics

# References and further reading

1   *Manufacture and Storage of Explosives Regulations
    2005* SI 2005/1082 The Stationery Office 2005
    ISBN 0 11 072764 9

2   *Manufacture and storage of explosives: Manufacture
    and Storage of Explosives Regulations 2005* L139
    HSE Books 2005 ISBN 0 7176 2816 7

3   *Carriage of Dangerous Goods and Use of
    Transportable Pressure Equipment Regulations 2004*
    SI 2004/568 The Stationery Office 2004
    ISBN 0 11 049063 0

4   *Firework (Safety) Regulations 1997* SI 1997/2294
    The Stationery Office 1997 ISBN 0 11 064962 1

5   *Firework (Safety) (Amendment) Regulations 2004*
    SI 2004/1372 The Stationery Office 2004
    ISBN 0 11 049315 X

6   BS 7114: 1988 *Fireworks* British Standards Institution
    *Part 1: Classification of fireworks* ISBN 0 58 017026 8
    *Part 2: Specification of fireworks* ISBN 0 58 017027 6
    *Part 3: Methods of test for fireworks*
    ISBN 0 58 017028 4

7   *Firework Regulations 2004* SI 2004/1836
    The Stationery Office 2004 0 11 049542 X

8   *Giving your own firework display: How to run and fire
    it safely* HSG124 (Second edition) HSE Books 2005
    ISBN 0 7176 6162 8

9   *The event safety guide: A guide to health, safety and
    welfare at music and similar events* HSG195 (Second
    edition) HSE Books 1999 ISBN 0 7176 2453 6

10  *Health and Safety at Work etc Act 1974 Ch37*
    The Stationery Office 1974 ISBN 0 10 543774 3

11  *Management of Health and Safety at Work Regulations
    1999* SI 1999/3242 The Stationery Office 1997
    ISBN 0 11 085625 2

12  *The Dangerous Substances in Harbour Areas
    Regulations 1987* SI 1987/37 The Stationery Office
    1987 ISBN 0 11 076037 9

13  Civil Aviation Authority CAP 736 *Guide for the
    Operation of Lasers, Searchlights and Fireworks in
    United Kingdom Airspace Version 1* The Stationery
    Office 2003 ISBN 0 8603 9956 7

14  *Managing crowds safely: A guide for organisers at
    events and venues* HSG154 (Second edition)
    HSE Books 2000 ISBN 0 7176 1834 X

15  *Reporting of Injuries, Diseases and Dangerous
    Occurrences Regulations 1995* SI 1995/3163
    The Stationery Office 1995 ISBN 0 11 053751 3

16  *Control of Noise at Work Regulations 2005*
    SI 2005/1643 The Stationery Office 2005
    ISBN 0 11 072984 6

17  *Disposal of explosives waste* Chemical Safety Guidance
    Note CS23 HSE Books 1999 ISBN 0 7176 1624 X

18  *Classification and Labelling of Explosives Regulations
    1983* SI 1983/1140 The Stationery Office 1983

19  *Working with ADR: an introduction to the carriage of
    dangerous goods by road 2004* Department for
    Transport 2004 ISBN 1 904763 47 2
    www.hse.gov.uk/pubns/cdg.pdf

20  *Five steps to risk assessment* Leaflet INDG163(rev2)
    HSE Books 2006 (single copy free or priced packs of
    10 ISBN 0 7176 6189 X) Web version:
    www.hse.gov.uk/pubns/indg163.pdf

21  *Local Government (Miscellaneous Provisions) Act 1982*
    C10 The Stationery Office 1982

22  *Private Places of Entertainment (Licensing) Act 1967*
    C19 The Stationery Office 1967

23  *Civic Government (Scotland) Act 1982* C45
    The Stationery Office 1982

# Further reading

*Fireworks and the law: A guide to those who manufacture, store, transport or use fireworks 1994* available from CBI Explosives Industry Group, 103 New Oxford Street, London WC1A 1DU Tel: 020 7395 8063

*Essentials of health and safety at work* (Fourth edition) HSE Books 2006 ISBN 0 7176 6179 2

Also visit the following websites for further information:

HSE: **www.hse.gov.uk**
Department of Trade and Industry: **www.dti.gov.uk**
Explosive Industry Group: **www.eig.org.uk**
**www.fireworksafety.co.uk**

While every effort has been made to ensure the accuracy of the references listed in this publication, their future availability cannot be guaranteed.

# Further information

HSE priced and free publications are available by mail order from HSE Books, PO Box 1999, Sudbury, Suffolk CO10 2WA Tel: 01787 881165 Fax: 01787 313995 Website: www.hsebooks.co.uk (HSE priced publications are also available from bookshops and free leaflets can be downloaded from HSE's website: www.hse.gov.uk.)

For information about health and safety ring HSE's Infoline Tel: 0845 345 0055 Fax: 0845 408 9566 Textphone: 0845 408 9577 e-mail: hse.infoline@natbrit.com or write to HSE Information Services, Caerphilly Business Park, Caerphilly CF83 3GG.

British Standards are available from BSI Customer Services, 389 Chiswick High Road, London W4 4AL Tel: 020 8996 9001  Fax: 020 8996 7001 e-mail: cservices@bsi-global.com Website: www.bsi-global.com

The Stationery Office publications are available from The Stationery Office, PO Box 29, Norwich NR3 1GN Tel: 0870 600 5522  Fax: 0870 600 5533 e-mail: customer.services@tso.co.uk Website: www.tso.co.uk (They are also available from bookshops.)

Printed and published by the Health and Safety Executive
C25     09/06